Pictorial Forest Lawn

FOREST LAWN MEMORIAL-PARK

GLENDALE 5, CALIFORNIA

Telephones: Cleveland 6-3131
Citrus 1-4151   Zenith 4151

A First Step Up Toward Heaven

BY BRUCE BARTON

NOTHING in Los Angeles gives me a finer thrill than Forest Lawn. The cemeteries of the world cry out men's utter hopelessness in the face of death. Their symbols are pagan and pessimistic; their damp precincts add a final horror to the grief of parting; their upkeep is neglected; their very atmosphere oppressive. Small wonder that men shun them even in the sunlight, and pass by with eyes averted, on the other side.

Forest Lawn alone is different. Here every tree and shrub and flower proclaims that:

> "Life is ever lord of death,
>
> And love can never lose its own."

Here happy couples come to be married in The Little Church of the Flowers. Here sorrow sees no ghastly monuments, but only life and hope. I like the statues of little children, stepping gaily into life like new souls into Heaven. I like the statues of beautiful women, and most of all I like big Moses, that giant among men, who did his work and lay down to slumber unafraid, sure that the God to whom he had talked would talk with him again.

Visitors come from everywhere; I could wish that they might go home to remodel their local cemeteries after the pattern of Forest Lawn—a noble resting place for the departed and a perpetual delight for those who live. Not until that happens will we be able to call ourselves a truly Christian nation.

For we worship a Master who loved and laughed; to whom little children flocked, and in whose presence sick people found new health and joy. A Master who, on the very night before His death, could say, "Be of good cheer; I have overcome the world," and "because I live, ye shall live also." Surely if this faith is real to us, our burying grounds should proclaim it in accents of beauty and power. The followers of a triumphant Master should sleep in grounds more lovely than those where they lived—a park so beautiful that it seems a bit above the level of this world, a first step up toward Heaven.

The Builder's Creed

I BELIEVE in a happy Eternal Life.

I believe those of us who are left behind should be glad in the certain belief that those gone before, who believed in Him, have entered into that happier Life.

I believe, most of all, in a Christ that smiles and loves you and me.

I therefore know the cemeteries of today are wrong, because they depict an end, not a beginning. They have consequently become unsightly stoneyards full of inartistic symbols and depressing customs; places that do nothing for humanity save a practical act, and that not well.

I therefore prayerfully resolve on this New Year's Day, 1917, that I shall endeavor to build Forest Lawn as different, as unlike other cemeteries as sunshine is unlike darkness, as Eternal Life is unlike death. I shall try to build at Forest Lawn a great park, devoid of mis-shapen monuments and other customary signs of earthly death, but filled with towering trees, sweeping lawns, splashing fountains, singing birds, beautiful statuary, cheerful flow-ers, noble memorial architecture with interiors full of light and color, and redolent of the world's best history and romances. I believe these things educate and uplift a community.

Forest Lawn shall become a place where lovers new and old shall love to stroll and watch the sunset's glow, planning for the future or reminiscing of the past; a place where artists study and sketch; where school teachers bring happy children to see the things they read of in books; where little churches invite, triumphant in the knowledge that from their pul-pits only words of Love can be spoken; where memorialization of loved ones in sculptured marble and pictorial glass shall be encouraged but controlled by acknowledged artists; a place where the sorrowing will be soothed and strengthened because it will be God's garden. A place that shall be protected by an immense Endowment Care Fund, the principal of which can never be expended—only the income therefrom used to care for and perpetuate this Garden of Memory.

This is the Builder's Dream; this is the Builder's Creed.

The Builder

NOTE: On New Year's Day, 1917, a man stood on a hilltop overlooking the small country cemetery of some fifty-five acres which had just been placed in his charge. He saw no buildings—only a patch of lawn with a few straggling headstones. Beyond the scant dozen acres of developed ground, the hillsides rose, sere and brown. In that moment, a vision came to the man of what this tiny "God's Acre" might become; and standing there, he made a promise to The Infinite. When he reached home, he put this promise into words and called it "The Builder's Creed." Today, Forest Lawn's almost three hundred acres are eloquent witness that The Builder kept faith with his soul.

THE BOARD OF TRUSTEES

2

THE BUILDER'S CREED

I BELIEVE IN A HAPPY ETERNAL LIFE.

I BELIEVE THOSE OF US WHO ARE LEFT BEHIND SHOULD BE
GLAD IN THE CERTAIN BELIEF THAT THOSE GONE BEFORE, WHO
BELIEVED IN HIM, HAVE ENTERED INTO THAT HAPPIER LIFE.

I BELIEVE, MOST OF ALL, IN A CHRIST THAT SMILES AND
LOVES YOU AND ME.

I THEREFORE KNOW THE CEMETERIES OF TODAY ARE WRONG,
BECAUSE THEY DEPICT AN END, NOT A BEGINNING. THEY HAVE
CONSEQUENTLY BECOME UNSIGHTLY STONEYARDS FULL OF IN-
ARTISTIC SYMBOLS AND DEPRESSING CUSTOMS; PLACES THAT
DO NOTHING FOR HUMANITY SAVE A PRACTICAL ACT, AND
THAT NOT WELL.

I THEREFORE PRAYERFULLY RESOLVE ON THIS NEW YEAR'S
DAY, 1917, THAT I SHALL ENDEAVOR TO BUILD FOREST LAWN
AS DIFFERENT, AS UNLIKE OTHER CEMETERIES AS SUNSHINE IS
UNLIKE DARKNESS, AS ETERNAL LIFE IS UNLIKE DEATH. I SHALL
TRY TO BUILD AT FOREST LAWN A GREAT PARK, DEVOID OF
MISSHAPEN MONUMENTS AND OTHER CUSTOMARY SIGNS OF
EARTHLY DEATH, BUT FILLED WITH TOWERING TREES, SWEEPING
LAWNS, SPLASHING FOUNTAINS, SINGING BIRDS, BEAUTIFUL STATUARY,
CHEERFUL FLOWERS, NOBLE MEMORIAL ARCHITECTURE WITH
INTERIORS FULL OF LIGHT AND COLOR, AND REDOLENT OF THE
WORLD'S BEST HISTORY AND ROMANCES.

I BELIEVE THESE THINGS EDUCATE AND UPLIFT A COMMUNITY.

FOREST LAWN SHALL BECOME A PLACE WHERE LOVERS NEW
AND OLD SHALL LOVE TO STROLL AND WATCH THE SUNSET'S
GLOW, PLANNING FOR THE FUTURE OR REMINISCING OF THE PAST,
A PLACE WHERE ARTISTS STUDY AND SKETCH, WHERE SCHOOL
TEACHERS BRING HAPPY CHILDREN TO SEE THE THINGS THEY READ
OF IN BOOKS, WHERE LITTLE CHURCHES INVITE, TRIUMPHANT
IN THE KNOWLEDGE THAT FROM THEIR PULPITS ONLY WORDS
OF LOVE CAN BE SPOKEN, WHERE MEMORIALIZATION OF LOVED
ONES IN SCULPTURED MARBLE AND PICTORIAL GLASS SHALL BE
ENCOURAGED BUT CONTROLLED BY ACKNOWLEDGED ARTISTS;
A PLACE WHERE THE SORROWING WILL BE SOOTHED AND
STRENGTHENED BECAUSE IT WILL BE GOD'S GARDEN. A PLACE
THAT SHALL BE PROTECTED BY AN IMMENSE ENDOWMENT CARE-
FUND, THE PRINCIPAL OF WHICH CAN NEVER BE EXPENDED - ONLY
THE INCOME THEREFROM USED TO CARE FOR AND PERPETUATE
THIS GARDEN OF MEMORY.

THIS IS THE BUILDER'S DREAM, THIS IS THE BUILDER'S CREED.

The Builder

The Entrance Gates

BEYOND graceful wrought-iron gates, the largest in the world, lie the sacred grounds of Forest Lawn, the world's first Memorial-Park. Founded on the belief that a cemetery should remove man's fear of oblivion and bolster his faith in immortality, it is a place of peaceful vistas, friendly old-world buildings and famous works of art. Just inside the gates, white ducks and swans swim gaily on the shimmering surface of a pool from whose banks may be seen the Administration Building, inspired by the Tudor architecture of Compton Wynyates, English manor house noted for its charm and picturesque beauty.

The Administration Building and Mortuary, Forest Lawn Memorial-Park

"God's Messenger," Forest Lawn Memorial-Park

UNLIKE other cemeteries as Life is unlike Death, Forest Lawn is founded on the principle of service to the living. No signs of sorrow linger in this beautiful Park where memorial tablets are laid flush with the lawn (right). Amid beautiful trees and lawns stretching away toward buildings constructed for the ages, the sheltering arms of privacy bring comfort and solace to heavy hearts.

The Great Mausoleum, Forest Lawn Memorial-Park

ERE, memory is enshrined eternally amid surroundings of beauty. It has been the ideal and achievement of "The Builder" to create a haven of peace and quiet, where people may come, some seeking inspiration in famous masterpieces of art, others finding consolation and an answer to life's problems amid the beauty of these sacred grounds. Here is crystallized the beauty wrought by God through the hands of men. In the presence of such inspiration, sadness and anguish give way to an appreciation of life's beauty, and the belief that Love lives forever, is reborn.

Entrance to the Administration Building and Mortuary, Forest Lawn Memorial-Park

To the right of Cathedral Drive, immediately upon entering Forest Lawn, is the Administration Building and Undertaking Establishment (above). A masterpiece of Tudor architecture inspired by the noted English manor house, Compton Wynyates, the combined buildings are set amid towering trees and foliage of verdant beauty. Just as Forest Lawn Memorial-Park differs from other cemeteries, so Forest Lawn Mortuary differs from other undertaking establishments. Here the sheltering arm of privacy surrounds both the departed and those who remain. The undertaking establishment is within a lovely, sacred park, secluded from the world about it by a high, ivy-covered wall. Within the building itself, the cheerful friendliness of quiet, sunlit rooms, looking out upon vistas of spiritual beauty, brings welcome comfort to heavy hearts. Here are complete seclusion, peaceful privacy and sacred services in sacred grounds. This is the kindlier, more reverent way.

The Shrine of Love, Forest Lawn Memorial-Park

"Family Love"

AT Forest Lawn, the love that links the living with the departed is fittingly perpetuated by "The Shrine of Love." Comprising three warmly human statuary groups which symbolize the great bond uniting those who remain with those who are gone, they are all originals by Ernesto Gazzeri. A detail of the central group, called "Family Love," is shown at the left.

The Church of the Recessional, Forest Lawn Memorial-Park

THE timeless symbols of eternal truths, Forest Lawn's three historic little churches bring to the new world the strength and courage of the old. Providing a dignified setting for final tribute, they serve also for the joyous and memorable ceremonies of christenings and the exchange of wedding vows. The largest church at Forest Lawn is The Church of the Recessional (above), a reproduction of ancient St. Margaret's in Rottingdean, England, where the soldier-poet Rudyard Kipling worshipped. It is a lasting memorial of the sentiments expressed in his famous poem, "The Recessional." Near by in Youth's Corner (left) the bronze statue of a boy symbolizes the thousands of young people who have found inspiration in the poem "If," inscribed on the stone plaque set in the high, ivy-covered wall.

IN a walled forecourt of The Church of the Recessional stands the romantic stone Ring of Aldyth through which bridal couples clasp hands and pledge their devotion. Below is a view of the Church interior. The words painted over the chancel arch, "Now abideth faith, hope, love, these three; and the greatest of these is love," express the Spirit of Forest Lawn and the imperishable creed of its three historic and regularly dedicated churches.

The Ring of Aldyth

Interior, The Church of the Recessional

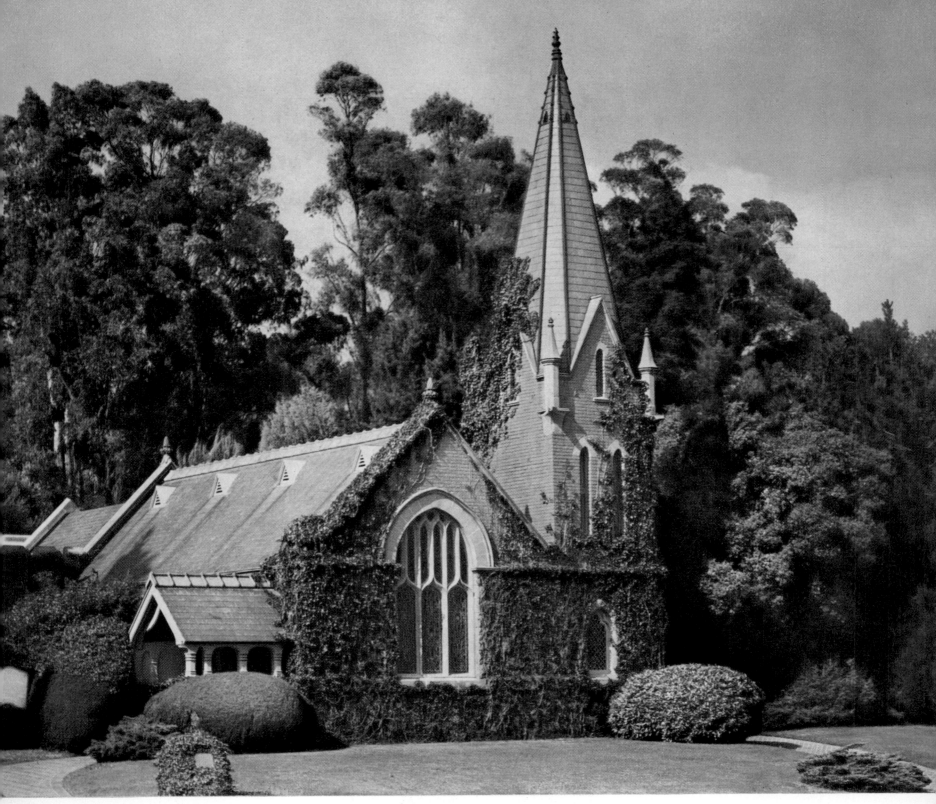

The Little Church of the Flowers, Forest Lawn Memorial-Park

ESTLING against a background of stately trees stands Forest Lawn's romantic, ivy-covered Little Church of the Flowers. With its sharp-pitched roof and slender spire, it is typical of the village churches of old England. It was inspired, indeed, by the quaint 14th Century church of Stoke Poges, in Slough, England, where Thomas Gray, 200 years ago, wrote his immortal "Elegy, Written in a Country Churchyard." The same old-world charm and peaceful atmosphere of its exterior is reflected in its interior as well. On each side of the nave are five arches framing quaint windows always banked with verdant ferns and the flowers which give the peaceful little church its name.

ON a spring morning some 25 years ago, a bride-to-be stood in The Little Church of the Flowers and exclaimed, "What a beautiful place for a wedding. I should love to be married here." Her wish was granted. And since that time, nearly 41,000 other happy people have been married in this and other Forest Lawn churches. All provide charming Brides' Rooms and Bridegrooms' Rooms. Near the entrance of each are kept the Wedding Records. The men and women whose names are listed there represent every State in the Union as well as a dozen foreign countries.

Bride's Room

Interior, The Little Church of the Flowers

The Wee Kirk o' the Heather, Forest Lawn Memorial-Park

IN a sheltering fold of a heather-flowered hillside stands the quaint **Wee Kirk o' the Heather** (above), a faithful reconstruction of Annie Laurie's own kirk in Glencairn. In the forecourt (right) stands the Wishing Chair, built of stones which once comprised a part of the original Scottish church. Thousands of happy couples have sat in this chair on their wedding day to recite together this translation of an old Scottish verse:

> Dressed in our best and all alone,
> We sit within the Wishing Chair
> Which bodes success for everyone
> Exchanging bridal kisses there.

14

Interior, The Wee Kirk o' the Heather

THE charm of the Scottish kirk has been so preserved in the interior of The Wee Kirk o' the Heather that the late Sir Harry Lauder, when he stepped inside it, remarked, "A wee bit o' dear aulde Scotland in California." Built from sketches found in an old Scottish library, The Wee Kirk is an exact reproduction of the original. One side of the nave is banked with growing greenery and flowers. On the other, windows tell in richly glowing colors the story of Annie Laurie's unrequited love for William Douglas. Photographs, letters and other items associated with the girl, whose face was "the fairest e'er the sun shone on," were brought from Glencairn, Scotland, and placed in the Historical Room near the entrance.

15

In God's Garden

GOD IN HIS BOUNDLESS LOVE HATH WROUGHT
THIS HOLY, QUIET, HALLOWED SPOT.
IN SHINING SUN AND TWILIGHT STILL
HE TEACHETH US TO KNOW HIS WILL.
AND IN THIS GARDEN SET APART
HE LAYETH PEACE UPON THE HEART
AND BRINGETH LOVED ONES TO US NEAR
AS HIS OWN HOLY PRESENCE HERE.
JAMES W. FOLEY.

A HAVEN for those who seek peace and meditation, "God's Garden" adjoining The Wee Kirk o' the Heather enshrines a smaller reproduction of Thorvaldsen's "The Christus." The poem inscribed on the stone plaque nearby expresses most eloquently the rewards that await those whose hearts reach out for the love and compassion of the Holy Saviour.

God's Garden, Forest Lawn Memorial-Park

Lullaby Land, Forest Lawn Memorial-Park

THE boundless power of God to create life and to sustain life throughout eternity is nowhere more forcibly expressed at Forest Lawn than in Babyland and Lullabyland. A tribute to the golden days of childhood, these portions of Forest Lawn are an enchanting memorial to the everlasting happiness in a child's heart. The Poem "Babyland," inscribed on plaques at both Lullabyland and Babyland, expresses in tender refrain the echoing memories of sweet and innocent childhood.

Babyland at Christmastime

Babyland

By E. A. BRININSTOOL

You strain your ears to catch a note
  That drifts, in cadence soft and low,
From out the Heaven Land remote,
  Where all the little children go.

And often, in your dreams, you hear
  In echoes gently, sweetly flung,
Some simple song, in accents clear,
  Your little one has often sung.

And so from out the Shadow-Shore,
  God hands to you the golden key,
With which you may unlock the door
  Of sacred, hallowed memory.

And from within, a smiling face
  Before your eager vision stands,
And you may feel the glad embrace
  Of dimpled, loving baby hands.

"Helping Hands"

"The Duck Baby"

IN the heart of a child, man may find the secret of the universe. That is why sculptured children romp the banks of the Duck Pool and find a home within the walls of this beautiful garden. Works of contemporary artists, they are fashioned of both bronze and marble. No one can see them without recalling the happy, carefree days of childhood, and the greater meaning that echoes in the words of Him who said, "And the little child shall enter in." In the joy of such works as Edith Barrett Parsons' "Duck Baby" and "Frog Baby," sorrow gives way to the certain knowledge that "life is ever lord of death."

"Sleepy Time"

"The Frog Baby"

"Happy Baby"

"The Battle of the Flowers"

"Motherly Tenderness"

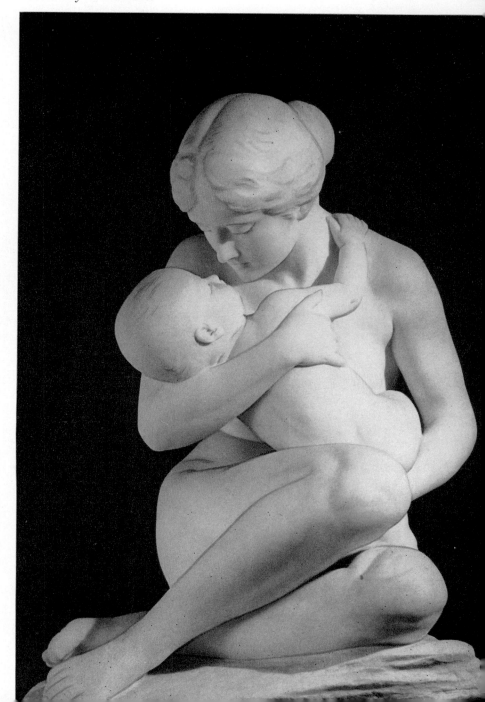

OREST LAWN'S outstanding statuary collection of winsome, playful children is augmented by several works which further embellish tender thoughts of the child. These comprise portrayals of the most tender of all subjects—glorious, idealized motherhood—which has served to inspire many artists throughout the ages. One example of this eternal theme is "Mother Love," an original by Saul Fantani who expressed in it the great love he bore for his models, his wife and their child.

FRAMED by ever-verdant trees, the Forest Lawn Mausoleum is one of the most impressive shrines of memory in the world. Its myriad sunlit corridors, constructed of the finest imported and domestic marbles, house one of America's finest collections of memorial art and sculpture. A great Endowment Care Fund protects and guards its maintenance. Situated on a height overlooking a sweep of fertile valley and blue mountains, the Forest Lawn Mausoleum is built solidly for all time. It is an ageless monument to beauty for those who would perpetuate in superb surroundings the memory of their loved ones.

The Upper Terraces of The Great Mausoleum, Forest Lawn Memorial-Park

The Great Mausoleum as seen from the air

INSPIRED by the world-famous Campo Santo in Genoa, Italy, the Great Mausoleum extends over nine massive terraces, yet convenient access is provided by entrances at many levels. Enough steel and concrete were used in its construction to erect an office building seventy stories high. Resistant to fire and earthquake, the Great Mausoleum is an achievement in permanence, protection and inspiring beauty—a monument built to stand forever.

"The Madonna of the Chair" Window

𝕿HE interior of the Great Mausoleum is alive with the light and beauty of memorial stained glass . . . an art that has endured through the centuries as one of the most lasting and expressive means of paying tribute to those we love. "Time cannot wither nor death destroy" the glory of mother love, so radiantly expressed in the "Madonna of the Chair" Window, a re-creation in stained glass of the immortal painting by Raphael. The original, painted in 1516 on the circular top of a wooden winecask, is in the Pitti Palace in Florence. This master-piece was among the great art treasures seized by the soldiers of Napoleon and removed to Paris, but was returned to Florence in 1815 and has been in the Pitti Palace ever since. At Forest Lawn, the enduring warmth of spiritual love is recaptured in this window brightening the entrance to Holly Terrace in the Great Mausoleum. Though Raphael's immortal Madonna has been copied in virtually every known form, none compares more faithfully with the original than this beautiful masterpiece in stained glass, executed by the world famous artist, Heinigke.

"I am the Alpha and Omega, the beginning and the end"—the triumphant
departure of Christ in majesty, pictured in stained glass by Nicola D'Ascenzo.

The Sanctuary of Valor

FOREST LAWN Sanctuaries, like the Sanctuary of Valor, proclaim the all-embracing and ever-enduring love of God. In the climaxing beauty of the Valor Window, the noble deeds of King Arthur's Knights of the Round Table in their courageous quest for the Holy Grail are retold in vibrant colors and designs through the distinctive stained glass artistry of Charles J. Connick.

The Paradise Sarcophagus

THE Paradise Sarcophagus (above), a distinctive family memorial in The Great Mausoleum, is graced with exact reproductions of panels from the famed Ghiberti doors, which Michelangelo once declared were "Worthy to be the gates of paradise." Love expressed in forms of beauty is deathless, for as the poet John Keats wrote: "A thing of beauty is a joy forever." This belief has prompted Forest Lawn to bring great statuary, architecture, and stained glass together in the unforgettable combination such as may be seen in the majestic Sanctuary of Heavenly Promise (right).

The Chancel Window, The Church of the Recessional
Forest Lawn Memorial-Park

THE Chancel Window of The Church of the Recessional is an exquisite representation in stained glass of the Virgin Mother and her Holy Child. This window is but one of Charles J. Connick's many artistic contributions to Forest Lawn's magnificent and world renowned collection of stained glass masterpieces.

THE radiant colors of stained glass go hand in hand with radiant memory, for at Forest Lawn, each window is a unique and individual expression of love. In D'Ascenzo's Good Shepherd Window (right) the basis of all earthly love is portrayed in the simple grandeur of the Eternal Love held by the Divine Shepherd for His sheep as He gathers them from the wilderness into the fold.

"Twilight Hush" Window

The Good Shepherd Window

FOREST Lawn's collection of stained glass is the finest in America. Totaling more than 360 windows of romantic and religious inspiration, it brings to life famous Bible stories, inspiring poetry and beloved memories. In gem-like colors that defy description the windows of Forest Lawn express joy, hope and love. Their radiant colors thrill. Their messages restore faith, dispel grief and gloom.

"Abide With Me" Window

THE beautiful Twilight Hush Window (left) created by the master, Charles Connick, takes as its theme the unforgettable lines from Whittier's poem "Eventide." "At this late hour—yet not unthankfully—I call to mind the fountains by the way." Equally beloved is the sentiment expressed in the "Abide With Me" Window (right), with the words, "O Thou who changest not, abide with me!"

$\mathbf{O}$NE of the tenderest emotions—memory —lives eternally in the radiant Memory Window, a masterpiece in stained glass through which the sunlight illuminates poet Thomas Hood's beloved words:

> "I remember, I remember,
> The house where I was born,
> The little window where the sun
> Came peeping in at morn."

Memory Window is the creation of Charles J. Connick, famed artist in stained glass. When he first saw it affixed in its beautiful setting, the sun blazing through the multicolored glass, he solemnly proclaimed it as his finest work.

The Memory Window

The Columbarium of Memory

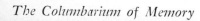

$\mathbf{S}$ORROW cannot exist where brightness and beauty abide. This is especially true of Forest Lawn's forty-three Columbaria. Here radiant stained glass windows and the soft blend of rare marbles lend warmth and tranquility to the Columbarium of Memory.

THE "Peace which passeth understanding" comforts the weary heart in the Corridor of the Madonna in the Great Mausoleum. Soft rays of the sun bathe graceful marble figures with cheery warmth. At the end of the corridor, keeping her vigil of love, stands the Madonna with the infant Jesus. This beautiful statuary piece is a recreation in pure cararra marble of Raphael's renowned and beloved painting "Madonna and Child."

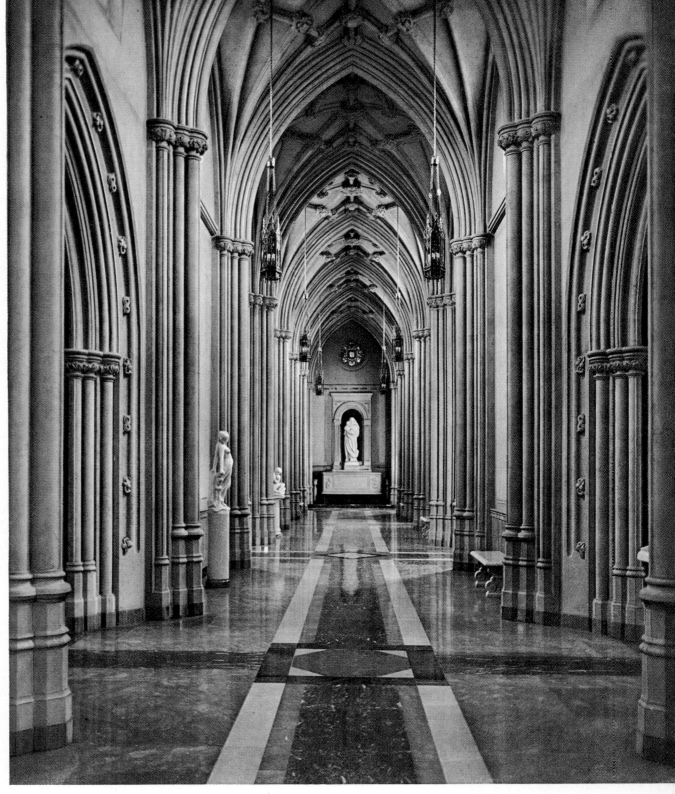

The Corridor of the Madonna

The Sanctuary of Celestial Peace

IN the beautiful marbles of the Great Mausoleum is a world of romance that brings the glory of many countries and civilizations together in hues and colors that are ageless, timeless, enduring. Carefully chosen and expertly placed, Forest Lawn's collection of priceless marbles has no counterpart. In the Great Mausoleum may be seen the rich burgundy of French Rouge Antique; the shell-like delicacy of creamy Botticino from the quarries of Italy; the rare beauty of Loredo Chiaro threaded extravagantly with startling garnet veins; the handsome and aristocratic pink-gray marble known as "Porta Santa," or "Portals of the Saints," so called because of its use in the basilicas of ancient Rome. These, the stones of eternity —from the United States, Spain, Greece, Belgium, France, Italy—all join together in a rare blend of beauty that reflects protection, warmth and everlasting memory.

"St. George," Forest Lawn Memorial-Park

Donatello's "St. George" is a symbol in flawless cararra marble of the very heart and soul of Forest Lawn for it was St. George, martyred Christian hero, who put faith and love of God before all else.

Memorial Court of Honor

Leonardo da Vinci

WHEN mortal man molds the expression of his thoughts on Immortality, he uses as his material the very symbols of Immortality itself. Of such timeless material was built The Memorial Court of Honor, Forest Lawn's beautiful shrine to the "Immortals"—those Americans whose great achievements serve as valuable and lasting contributions to humanity. Situated in the Great Mausoleum, the Memorial Court of Honor is a room of great size bathed with softly diffused tints as sunlight penetrates the stained glass of "The Last Supper" Window. This rare masterpiece, a re-creation of Leonardo da Vinci's greatest painting, dominates the beauty of the great court, and treasures of fine art. Here, too, are exact re-creations from original works of the master sculptor, Michelangelo. Bordering one wall are his two companion groups, "Twilight and Dawn" and "Night and Day," while facing them along the opposite wall are "La Pieta" and "Medici Madonna and Child," all originally created in the Sixteenth Century.

Memorial Court of Honor is vaulted by graceful medieval cathedral arches. The blue of the arched ceiling, soaring fifty feet above the floor, seems to open the court to the skies. High overhead are other windows of stained glass while below them are imposing walls of warmly blended colors, lending a fitting background to the white marble statuary.

Although Memorial Court of Honor is an artistic masterpiece, its beauty does not overshadow its purpose—the foundation for a "Westminster Abbey of the New World" where honored entombment of distinguished Americans may serve as perpetual reward for great service to all generations.

Here, beneath its resplendent "The Last Supper" Window, are crypts which no amount of money can buy. They are held in special trust for use only when Forest Lawn's Council of Regents bestows the title of "Immortal" on one of great and lasting achievements.

Such an honor is granted only after careful and exhaustive deliberation by the Council of Regents. Thus far only two have been so honored. The first was Gutzon Borglum, the gifted sculptor who turned the Black Hills of South Dakota into a "Shrine of Democracy" by carving four gigantic heads of Washington, Jefferson, Lincoln and Theodore Roosevelt from the living granite of Mount Rushmore.

The second was Carrie Jacobs-Bond, a gallant mother whose gentle songs of love and faith have become traditions in American music. "I Love You Truly," "A Perfect Day" and a hundred more were written in a language of the heart understood by all.

The Memorial Court of Honor is a scene of majestic serenity, of quiet beauty, of uplifting inspiration—truly a fitting tribute to God and to Man as a creature of God.

Rosa Caselli Moretti

Memorial Court of Honor, Forest Lawn Memorial-Park

MT. RUSHMORE, SOUTH DAKOTA

GUTZON BORGLUM
1871 SCULPTOR 1941

HIS BIRTHPLACE WAS IDAHO. CALIFORNIA FIRST TAUGHT HIM ART. THEN FRANCE WHO FIRST GAVE HIM FAME. HIS GENIUS FOR THE EXQUISITE AS FOR THE COLOSSAL GAVE PERMANENCE IN BRONZE AND MARBLE TO MOODS OF BEAUTY OR PASSION, TO FIGURES OF LEGEND AND HISTORY. AS PATRIOT HE STRIPPED CORRUPTION BARE. AS STATESMAN HE TOILED FOR EQUALITY IN THE RIGHTS OF MAN. AT LAST HE CARVED A MOUNTAIN FOR A MONUMENT. HE MADE THE MOUNTAIN CHANT: "REMEMBER! THESE GIANT SOULS SET AMERICA FREE AND KEPT HER FREE. HOLD FAST YOUR SACRED HERITAGE, AMERICANS! REMEMBER! REMEMBER!"

Rupert Hughes

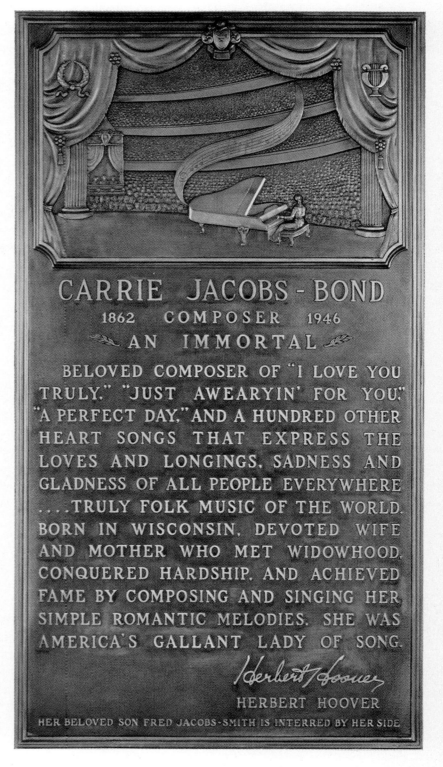

CARRIE JACOBS - BOND
1862 COMPOSER 1946
AN IMMORTAL

BELOVED COMPOSER OF "I LOVE YOU TRULY." "JUST AWEARYIN' FOR YOU." "A PERFECT DAY." AND A HUNDRED OTHER HEART SONGS THAT EXPRESS THE LOVES AND LONGINGS, SADNESS AND GLADNESS OF ALL PEOPLE EVERYWHERE ....TRULY FOLK MUSIC OF THE WORLD. BORN IN WISCONSIN, DEVOTED WIFE AND MOTHER WHO MET WIDOWHOOD. CONQUERED HARDSHIP, AND ACHIEVED FAME BY COMPOSING AND SINGING HER SIMPLE ROMANTIC MELODIES. SHE WAS AMERICA'S GALLANT LADY OF SONG.

Herbert Hoover

HERBERT HOOVER

HER BELOVED SON FRED JACOBS-SMITH IS INTERRED BY HER SIDE

CAST in imperishable bronze and bearing at its top a bas-relief of the gigantic Mount Rushmore Memorial that made him famous, is a bronze plaque marking the resting place of Gutzon Borglum, the first person ever to be entombed as an Immortal of Memorial Court of Honor. Borglum was a sculptor with tools mightier than chisel and mallet. His tools were democracy, tolerance, freedom and happiness, the great ideals of America. For his noble expression of eternal values he was granted entombment beneath "The Last Supper" Window.

THE memorial plaque honoring Carrie Jacobs-Bond, second person to be accorded honored entombment as an Immortal of Memorial Court of Honor, bears a bas-relief of the gentle composer in her most characteristic pose—singing and playing her songs. Hushed in rapt attention, her vast audience listens enthralled at the simple, stirring melodies. The notes rise to become part of a universal melody. Because her noble simplicity won the hearts of people everywhere, Forest Lawn's Council of Regents granted her this place, in Memorial Court of Honor.

"The Last Supper" Window

IN Forest Lawn's breath-taking re-creation in stained glass of "The Last Supper," a masterpiece has been saved for civilization. Occupying the north end of Memorial Court of Honor it preserves for all time Leonardo da Vinci's interpretation of the most dramatic scene in the life of the most dramatic character ever to step from the pages of History.

The original, painted by the genius Leonardo on the walls of a convent in Milan, Italy, is unanimously declared to be one of the greatest paintings the world has ever known.

But the centuries have taken their toll. This priceless picture has decayed and fallen away until the original work is almost obliterated. Despite the modern, scientific knowledge at his command, man has been unable to thwart the ceaseless ravages of time.

During World War II, the convent of Santa Maria delle Grazie was badly damaged by bombs. The nave was struck and the refectory containing "The Last Supper" was almost completely destroyed. Although the wall bearing the painting was not damaged, the painting itself suffered even further deterioration from sandbags placed against it for its protection.

The day when its fading colors are finally extinguished is not far off. But when it comes, this most treasured of art wor[k]
Forest Lawn, in "The Last Supper" W[indow]
re-created, not from the dimmed mura[l]
sketches. Here, in glorious and imperish[able]
painter and the comforting message of t[he]

The Biblic[al]

The scene portrayed in "The Last S[upper]
Matthew, Chapter 26.

Now when the even was come, He sat [down]
eat, He said, Verily I say unto you, tha[t]
were exceedingly sorrowful, and bega[n]
Lord, is it I? And He answered and s[aid]
in the dish, the same shall betray Me.

The Son of Man goeth as it is written o[f]
the Son of Man is betrayed! It had b[een good for that man if he had not]
been born.

Then Judas, which betrayed Him, ansv[ered and said]
unto him, Thou hast said.

t be lost to the world. For at
e great painting lives anew—
m Leonardo da Vinci's own
d glass, the genius of a Master
scene defy the ages.

s chosen from the Book of

the twelve. And as they did
u shall betray Me. And they
of them to say unto Him,
t dippeth his hand with Me

woe unto that man by whom
for that man if he had not

said, Master, is it I? He said

*Explanatory Diagram of Figures in
"The Last Supper" Window*

(1) Bartholomew springs to his feet in amazement; (2) James the Lesser touches the shoulder of the enraged Peter; (3) Andrew shrinks from Judas whom he suspects as the betrayer; (4) Judas, clutching his money bag, overturns the salt; (5) Peter angrily awaits the betrayer's name; (6) John is overcome by the startling words; (7) Thomas, the doubter, expresses his disbelief; (8) James the Greater is horrified at the accusation; (9) Philip asks "Is it I, Master?"; (10) Matthew asks Simon if he, too, has heard this accusation; (11) Thaddeus frowns as he looks accusingly toward Judas; (12) Simon is amazed at His words.

EXPLANATORY DIAGRAM

IT was Professor Armando Vene, Royal Superintendent of Fine Arts of Italy, who pointed out that Forest Lawn is the only place in the world where all of Michelangelo's greatest works are gathered together in one place. By making this possible, he added, Forest Lawn has performed a notable service to humanity. At the right is "Madonna of Bruges" and below is an exact reproduction of his "Twilight and Dawn," the original of which is in the Medici Chapel in Florence. Both can be found in beautiful Memorial Court of Honor. An allegory in marble, "Twilight and Dawn" depicts the mind of man. Dawn, the female figure, portrays the mind as it tries to fathom the true significance of life, while the male figure, Twilight, symbolizes that time when the mind discerns the intentions and will of God through the veil of life.

"Madonna of Bruges"

"Twilight and Dawn"

"Day and Night"

"Medici Madonna and Child"

MICHELANGELO, master sculptor of all time, in his ninety years of achievement created works which have inspired mankind for more than four centuries. His figures of "Day and Night" (above) illustrate the incomparable breadth of his vision and genius. Day is the virile masculine figure, alert and alive. Night is the graceful female figure who sleeps, in confidence of a glorious awakening. The sublime strength in these powerful figures gives way to sublime tenderness in the "Medici Madonna" (right). A reproduction of the original which stands in the Medici Chapel in Florence, Italy, it depicts the warmest of all earthly emotions—the tender love of a mother for her child.

"Moses"

T the entrance to Cathedral Corridor in Memorial Terrace stands the only exact, full size reproduction of Michelangelo's magnificent statue of "Moses," the Deliverer, who led the children of Israel out of bondage. It was through Moses that God made known to man His Commandments, and Moses gave to the world an immortal example of the power of faith. Though there are many copies of this statue, Forest Lawn's is the only one cast from clay masks placed directly on the original statue in the Church of Saint Peter in Chains at Rome, Italy.

"La Pieta"

LA PIETA, created by Michelangelo when but a youth, glorifies in marble the infinite tenderness with which the Mother holds the body of Her Crucified Son. Truly, Christ's sacrifice was at once the Virgin Mary's sacrifice . . . but in Her face is seen only supreme confidence that in death is eternal life, and that which is lost to the world of man becomes immortal in the Kingdom of God. Forest Lawn's reproduction, made from the original in St. Peter's Cathedral in Rome, is enshrined in Memorial Court of Honor as an unforgettable testimony to faith.

FOREST Lawn's exact reproduction of Michelangelo's colossal statue of "David" towers twenty and a half feet above Dr. Rufus B. von KleinSmid, Chancellor of the University of Southern California, and Dr. Hubert Eaton, Chairman of the Board of Forest Lawn, who are shown at the time of its official unveiling before distinguished civic and religious leaders.

THE story of Forest Lawn unfolds not only in beautiful buildings and churches, but in unique outdoor courts where magnificent statuary may stand against the majestic canopy of nature. Such a place is The Court of David, high atop Mount Forest Lawn. David's glorious victory over the giant Philistine, Goliath, is retold in one of three heavy bronze bas-relief plaques (right) which embellish the beautiful wall of native stone encompassing The Court of David. Here is the perfect setting, high on a hilltop open to the sky, for the heroic young champion of Israel (below). Carved from pure white cararra marble exactly as Michelangelo so masterfully chiseled the original, the towering statue of David stands in simple glory, as he must have so many centuries ago when he faced the giant Philistine and conquered him.

The "David and Goliath" Plaque

The Court of David, Forest Lawn Memorial-Park

FROM a lowly beginning to the height of power through faith in God! That is the inspiring story of Moses, the first chapter of which is portrayed in The Finding of Moses Fountain. Below is Forest Lawn's re-creation of the original setting as it appears in Rome, even to the sprays of water and planting of nearby trees. At left is a close-up showing the daughter of Pharaoh, her face radiant at the discovery of the infant. Long a favorite masterpiece among the children of Rome, this fountain and the Bible story it illustrates are equally beloved by the little children of Southern California.

The Finding of Moses Fountain

"Protection"

"Hallowed Hours"

BROWN

CAPTAIN DON EVAN
1915 – 1942

MAN'S noblest instinct, the preservation of his family, is the theme of the memorable bronze original shown above. The dramatic work of Mario Moschi, it is fittingly called "Protection." At left is "Hallowed Hours," the final work of the great Italian sculptor, Amleto Cataldi. Like "Protection," the group is an original; each surmounts a family sarcophagus of fine marble.

43

ON the summit of a gently sloping crest overlooking the verdant acres of Forest Lawn, is The Mystery of Life Garden, a specially designed, walled garden landscaped with rare shrubs and trees. Here stands "The Mystery of Life" statuary group flanked by other statues depicting joyous blessings of life.

A NUMBER of family memorials embellish the inspiring beauty of The Mystery of Life Garden, among them the stirring statuary group, "Family Affection," shown above. Below is a view of this green vista of peace enhanced by God's delicate handiwork of sunlight and shade.

The Mystery of Life Garden, Forest Lawn Memorial-Par

"A Child's Prayer"

IN the garden which bears its name is "The Mystery of Life" statuary group, one of the most beautiful allegories ever shaped in marble. Depicting the eighteen stages of man's development, it is the work of the noted sculptor, Ernesto Gazzeri, who carved it expressly for Forest Lawn. At right is another of the garden's statues, "A Child's Prayer" by Lazzerini, a portrayal of the soft voice sending its message of love and devotion toward Heaven.

"The Mystery of Life," Forest Lawn Memorial-Park

The Story of "The Mystery of Life"

AROUND the mystic Stream of Life we see grouped eighteen persons typifying many walks and stations of life. First we see (1) a boy, who is astonished at the miracle that has happened in his hand—one moment, an unbroken egg; the next moment, a chick, teeming with life. "Why?" he asks. "How does it happen? What is the answer to this Mystery of Life?" He questions (2) his aged grandmother, who, he reasons, knows everything. But we see her resigned in the face of the inexplicable. Then we see (3 and 4) the lovers, who believe they have found the answer to the mystery in their first kiss; (5) the sweet girl graduate, lost in dreams, with no place as yet in her thoughts for a serious questioning of life's destiny; (6) the scientist, troubled because all his learning, all his searchings, have not solved the mystery; (7 and 8) the mother, who finds the answer in the babe at her breast; (9, 10, 11, 12, 13) the happy family group, not greatly perturbed by the mystery, although even they seem to ask, "Why do the doves mate?"

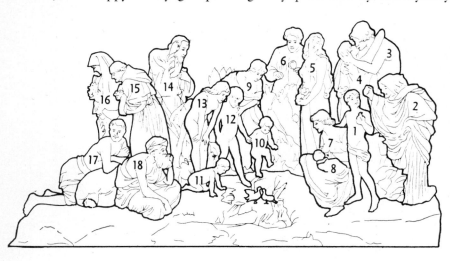

(14) the learned philosopher, scratching his puzzled head in vain; (15 and 16) the monk and the nun, comforted and secure, confident they have found the answer in their religion; (17) the atheist, the fool, who grinningly cares not at all; while (18) the stoic sits in silent awe and contemplation of that which he believes he knows but cannot explain with any satisfaction. Here is but one explanation of "The Mystery of Life" group, a masterpiece defying any exact interpretation. Do you see yourself in one of the characters here portrayed? Each one who studies it should form his own interpretation of the symbols of the greatest mystery.

The Gardens of Memory

EMBELLISHED with inspiring statuary and beautifully landscaped with trees, lawns and flowering shrubs, Forest Lawn's revolutionary "Gardens of Memory" demonstrate once again its leadership among cemeteries of the world. Here, for the first time anywhere, are memorial sanctuaries designed for families who desire the privacy and protection of crypt interment, but who at the same time long for the open skies and the natural beauty of a verdant garden bathed in sunlight. Under the lawns in the Gardens of Memory have been created a number of monolithically constructed crypts of steel-reinforced concrete. Offering all the protection heretofore obtainable only in the Mausoleum, yet they are set out in God's own earth, beneath sun and stars. Surrounded with friendly, ivy-covered walls of natural stone, the gardens offer sanctuary to the spirit, remembrance to the heart and true assurance that here is the perfect and everlasting tribute.

The Gardens of Memory, Forest Lawn Memorial-Park

Doorway, The Gardens of Memory

SET in one of Forest Lawn's picturesque walls of natural stone is a graceful door of massive bronze, unlocked by golden keys presented only to those whose interment property lies within the peaceful Gardens of Memory beyond. Near this unique door, framed by leafy garlands, is a bronze plaque inscribed with endearing words of the poem, "Death is Only an Old Door." Below is shown a typical family garden of comforting privacy found in the Gardens of Memory, a quiet refuge of rest, peace and solace.

The Little Garden of Friendship

"Abraham Lincoln" by Augustus Saint-Gaudens

$\mathfrak{T}$HE Forest Lawn Museum, famed for its collection of great statuary and art objects, stands atop Mount Forest Lawn, adjoining The Hall of The Crucifixion. Redolent of the spirit pervading its sunlit halls is Augustus Saint-Gauden's original bronze of President Abraham Lincoln. One of the finest portrait statues in America, this familiar work perpetuates our national tribute to the leaders who helped make America a great nation.

49

"Appeal to the Great Spirit," by Cyrus Edwin Dallin

"Bronco Buster," by Frederick Remington

THE Forest Lawn Museum, where are preserved the great artistic achievements that have become our national heritage, is another way Forest Lawn fulfills its appointed task of Service to the Living. It enshrines a world-famous collection of original works by the most renowned American sculptors. The Roll of Honor includes such names as Daniel Chester French, Gutzon Borglum, Henry Hering, Frederick MacMonnies, James Earle Fraser, Frederick Remington. Here, in original pieces molded by their immortal hands, are simple human figures, symbolizing the broad sweep of American life, united in distinguished assembly with great men of all time.

"Mark Twain"
by Gladys Lewis Bush

"Theodore Roosevelt"
by James Earle Fraser

"Pro Patria"
Henry Hering

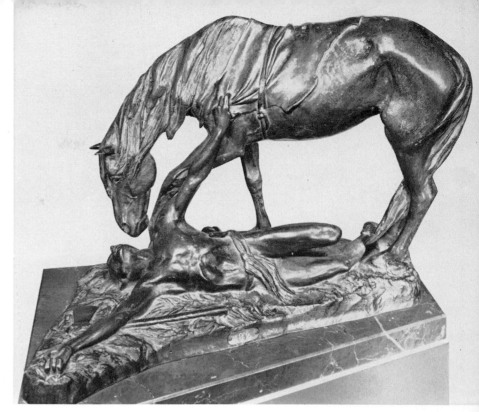

"Return of the Boer"
by Gutzon Borglum

"The Dying Chief"
by Gutzon Borglum

AMERICAN history is not the history of one man, or two, or a thousand times two. It is the history of a great people from whose ranks came leaders who could inspire because they understood the spirit of America. In the Forest Lawn Art Museum, they live again in original bronze sculptures by great American artists. Here is the citizen soldier, Nathan Hale, progenitor of every man who has left his home and the comforts of peace to defend his country. Here too are the lifelike bronze figures of Henry Clay, Daniel Webster, Theodore Roosevelt, Mark Twain, and many others whose hearts and minds endowed America with her unconquerable spirit.

"Nathan Hale"
by Frederick W. MacMonnies

"Henry Clay"
by Thomas Ball

"Daniel Webster"
by Thomas Ball

The Hall of History, Forest Lawn Memorial-Park

The Hall of History

"Lives of great men all remind us
We can make our lives sublime,
And departing leave behind us
Footprints on the sands of time."

THOSE unforgettable words of the poet Longfellow, inscribed in gold in The Hall of History at Forest Lawn, keynote this place dedicated to the history of Freedom and Democracy. Within the walls of The Hall of History, beats the pulse of America's greatness. In its collection of art treasures are statues, paintings and other memorabilia of the strong hands that guided this country's course in its hours of crisis. Lined with the rich burgundy of imported French Rouge Antique marble, The Hall of History is one of the most colorful rooms in The Great Mausoleum. On either side, through open windows the verdant, evergreen vistas of Forest Lawn stretch away like a velvety green carpet. This is indeed the perfect setting for a noble hall and its priceless treasures of American history. A real and constant inspiration to young and old alike, Forest Lawn's Hall of History is a shrine to the nobility and greatness of the United States of America, and the courageous men and women who helped create it.

IN the northwest corner of The Hall of History is a memorial dedicated to one of the greatest Americans of this era, General Charles Gates Dawes, former Vice President of the United States, and Ambassador to Great Britain. A tribute to General Dawes is inscribed on the stone tablet (right). The Dawes Memorial is a permanent witness to the magnificent leadership of such men as Abraham Lincoln, the Great Emancipator. In the original painting "Lincoln at Gettysburg" by Fletcher Ransom (below), one may almost hear the words, "Fourscore and seven years ago, our fathers brought forth upon this continent a new nation, conceived in liberty and dedicated to the proposition that all men are created equal."

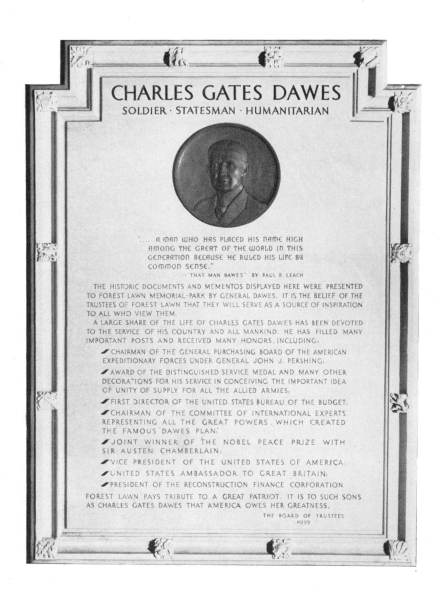

CHARLES GATES DAWES
SOLDIER · STATESMAN · HUMANITARIAN

"..... A MAN WHO HAS PLACED HIS NAME HIGH AMONG THE GREAT OF THE WORLD IN THIS GENERATION BECAUSE HE RULED HIS LIFE BY COMMON SENSE."
-- "THAT MAN DAWES" BY PAUL R. LEACH

THE HISTORIC DOCUMENTS AND MEMENTOS DISPLAYED HERE WERE PRESENTED TO FOREST LAWN MEMORIAL-PARK BY GENERAL DAWES. IT IS THE BELIEF OF THE TRUSTEES OF FOREST LAWN THAT THEY WILL SERVE AS A SOURCE OF INSPIRATION TO ALL WHO VIEW THEM.

A LARGE SHARE OF THE LIFE OF CHARLES GATES DAWES HAS BEEN DEVOTED TO THE SERVICE OF HIS COUNTRY AND ALL MANKIND. HE HAS FILLED MANY IMPORTANT POSTS AND RECEIVED MANY HONORS, INCLUDING:

- CHAIRMAN OF THE GENERAL PURCHASING BOARD OF THE AMERICAN EXPEDITIONARY FORCES UNDER GENERAL JOHN J. PERSHING;
- AWARD OF THE DISTINGUISHED SERVICE MEDAL AND MANY OTHER DECORATIONS FOR HIS SERVICE IN CONCEIVING THE IMPORTANT IDEA OF UNITY OF SUPPLY FOR ALL THE ALLIED ARMIES;
- FIRST DIRECTOR OF THE UNITED STATES BUREAU OF THE BUDGET;
- CHAIRMAN OF THE COMMITTEE OF INTERNATIONAL EXPERTS, REPRESENTING ALL THE GREAT POWERS, WHICH CREATED THE FAMOUS 'DAWES PLAN';
- JOINT WINNER OF THE NOBEL PEACE PRIZE WITH SIR AUSTEN CHAMBERLAIN;
- VICE PRESIDENT OF THE UNITED STATES OF AMERICA;
- UNITED STATES AMBASSADOR TO GREAT BRITAIN;
- PRESIDENT OF THE RECONSTRUCTION FINANCE CORPORATION.

FOREST LAWN PAYS TRIBUTE TO A GREAT PATRIOT. IT IS TO SUCH SONS AS CHARLES GATES DAWES THAT AMERICA OWES HER GREATNESS.
THE BOARD OF TRUSTEES
1939

"Lincoln at Gettysburg"   Fletcher C. Ransom

NOT EVERY man may endow a museum or a college, but at Forest Lawn, all may share in a greater, more beautiful, more enduring memorial than any one individual or one family could hope to create in the name of memory. It is a memorial that speaks out in the beauty of such family memorials as The Temple of Santa Sabina, formerly in the Basilica of Santa Sabina, one of the oldest Catholic Churches in Rome. It is a memorial that pays witness to the encompassing love of Christ for man, through such lovely statuary as "For of Such is the Kingdom of Heaven."

The Temple of Santa Sabina

"For of Such is the Kingdom of Heaven"

...FOR OF SUCH IS THE KINGDOM OF HEAVEN.

IN the majestic Court of The Christus near the summit of Mount Forest Lawn stands an exact reproduction of Bertel Thorvaldsen's world-renowned statue, "The Christus." A cascading waterfall rises at the feet of "The Christus" and disappears into the ground to reappear as the Stream of Life at "The Mystery of Life" statuary group in an adjacent court. There, it flashes briefly in the sun and once again returns to its source at the feet of "The Christus," symbolizing that Christ is, as He said, "The Alpha and Omega," the Beginning and the End—the Answer to The Mystery of Life.

55

The Hall of

CROWNING the peak of Mount Forest Lawn as though beckoning with gestures symbolic of hope and faith is the imposing Hall of The Crucifixion, a massive building entrusted with the sacred guardianship of a masterpiece without parallel anywhere.

This is the great structure which had to be built. Without it America's largest religious painting could not be displayed, for inside its bold but simple walls is enshrined "The Crucifixion"—a portrayal by Jan Styka of one of the most dramatic moments ever witnessed by the world.

So large is this magnificent and awe-inspiring masterpiece that for many years it could not be shown because no structure was large enough to house it. When it first came to the attention of the one man, Dr. Hubert Eaton, "The Builder" of Forest Lawn, who dared meet the challenge of its tremendous size, it was already a legend and few believed such a huge painting could actually exist. Only through the untiring efforts of Dr. Eaton was it finally found. This was to become the second event in the sacred trilogy, three great moments in the Life of Christ, which "The Builder" had pledged to Forest Lawn. The first event had been the placing of the stained glass re-creation of Leonardo da Vinci's beloved "The Last Supper" painting in Memorial Court of Honor. The second was to be this portrayal of the Lord's sacrifice on the cross. The third event is yet to come, the "Smiling Christ" after the Resurrection, the glorious climax to the trilogy.

Artist's Sketch of The Hall of The Crucifixion at Completion
Forest Lawn Memorial-Park

The Crucifixion

When the painting was first unrolled before the eyes of Dr. Eaton he was stunned by its emotional impact. He knew that Forest Lawn must mold its destiny. The Council of Regents unanimously agreed with great enthusiasm.

Yet how would it be displayed? Its size was staggering—45 feet in height and 195 feet in length. Not even the largest auditorium in existence was capable of its exhibition. Immediately Dr. Eaton ordered construction of a huge hall conceived in great simplicity, composed in mood, and strong, as though aware of its mission.

The steel and concrete walls are bold and impressive. A gigantic doorway opens into a concourse vaulted with cathedral arches. An oak-paneled corridor leads to the vestibule itself. Here is the broad sweep of seats, richly upholstered in burgundy, rising tier above tier, matching the splendor of the architecture.

The curtain which completely covers one vast wall of the huge auditorium was specially woven of velvet and hemmed by hand. Believed to be the world's largest curtain, it weighs more than three thousand pounds.

The majesty of The Hall of The Crucifixion is exceeded only by the majesty of the gigantic painting it enshrines. It is a monument to the great message contained in that painting. To those who pilgrimage to its doors in search of that message it is a shrine where inspiration is renewed in hope, in solace and in peace.

"The Crucifixion" Forest Lawn Memorial-Park, Glendale, California

"The Crucifixion"

An Interpretation

Curiosity bent, the people are seen streaming to the top of the hill from every gate in the city. The sky is overcast with sullen, leaden clouds and the pilgrims coming from the north report ominous rumblings of thunder in the hills.

These are also legal events, and the Roman rulers make certain that everything is done according to the letter of the law. Between the two crosses in the rear is Stephanus (13) the warrant officer, reading the orders of execution. His voice reaches Joseph of Arimathea (1), who stands at the edge of the cliff. Later on, he will beg the body of the Crucified Christ from the authorities so that he may place it in his own tomb. With Joseph is Nicodemus (2), a wealthy merchant. He knows and loves Jesus, but with all his wealth he is powerless to save him.

Between these friends of Jesus and the left-hand cross are gathered the members of the Sanhedrin, in their rich, official robes. The two men who bribed Judas to betray Christ are Annas (5), the former high priest, and his son-in-law, Caiaphus (6), the acting high priest. This is their hour of triumph. Now they await the death of their sworn enemy. Standing apart from the triumphant priests is Gamaliel (4),

the influential lawyer. Though a member of the Sanhedrin, he keeps well apart from the others for he is known to be sympathetic to the teachings of Jesus. Talking with Gamaliel is his pupil, Saul of Tarsus (3). Standing alone near the left-hand cross is Malchus (7), whose ear was struck off in fury by Simon Peter at the scene of the betrayal. Standing silent, eyes fixed upon Jesus, he wonders "What manner of man is this who heals one sent to destroy Him?" Over in the crowd to the right of the cross is Peter (22) staring aghast at a cock fluttering on the ground before him. Through the long night, while the priests and elders questioned and taunted Jesus, Peter three times denied his Lord as Jesus had prophesied he would. After the third denial a cock crowed, and the conscience-stricken Peter, remembering, weeps bitterly.

The time is growing short. The centurion Longinus (21) mounted on a white horse, shouts orders to have the riffraff turned back. He is uneasy at this scene because he has openly admitted his belief in Jesus, and history records him the first Roman to embrace the Christian faith.

In the center background, in front of a battalion of soldiers,

The Story of "The Crucifixion"

FEW artists have attempted to unfold the entire length and breadth of an all-encompassing drama that changed the course of the world that day on Golgotha. Yet Jan Styka, masterful artist of intense zeal and driving energy, not only attempted it, but successfully completed "The Crucifixion" on an enormous scale almost unbelievable in scope.

So huge, yet so meticulously executed down to the smallest detail, this tremendous painting has a strange and wondrous story. In many ways its history parallels the life of Him whose final hours before Crucifixion are interpreted by Styka—it was born of great promise, lived a brief life that brought hope and love to so many, then died only to be reborn in a new and greater existence for the ages.

Its history was written over a period of more than fifty years by a pen dipped in the work, the dreams, the genius of three men. The first chapter began in 1894 when Ignace Jan Paderewski, already a musician of note, stood before a gigantic painting depicting the struggle for Poland's freedom a century earlier. Into his mind came the idea for an even larger and greater painting, the subject to have not national, but universal meaning. He met the artist and found common ground in emotion and understanding, for both were intensely patriotic citizens of Poland; both were destined to be great artists. The plan was created.

While a gigantic canvas was made to order by Belgian weavers, the artist journeyed to the Holy Land—to the ancient, walled city of Jerusalem where he saw for himself the hill of Golgotha and re-created in his own mind the tragedy that occurred there two thousand years earlier. He sketched the hill, the city. He drew the characters, using as his models the people born within the very walls whose gates had opened to the condemned Christ.

On his return home he stopped in Rome, where he had once been a student, and knelt before Pope Leo XIII who blessed his palette—the same palette on display today in the Hall of the Crucifixion wherein is enshrined the painting that grew from the colors mixed on it. His welcome home in Lemberg, Poland, was triumphant.

The city officials granted him the use of a mammoth public building in which the huge canvas was hung from iron bars erected for it in the vaulted ceiling. Then Styka began his labor of love. For thousands of hours he worked, often far into the night in a deep religious fervor.

With amazing thoroughness, Styka completed his masterpiece of unparalleled authenticity. More than one thousand figures were there, characters greater than life size. And there were the important landmarks of the city itself.

Many times had the Crucifixion been depicted in oils but none such as this. Instead of the agonies of the Cross, Styka chose that moment of great suspense just before the Crucifixion when Christ stood among friends and enemies, praying quietly to His Father, unmindful of the cruel, mortal pain he must yet endure. The finished painting was greeted with great acclaim. Though "The Crucifixion" was displayed but briefly in Europe, the throngs who saw it were enthralled by its spiritual message. Then in 1900, Styka brought "The Crucifixion" to America. But no building or museum could accommodate the mammoth painting. In the disappointing months that followed, the despairing artist lost possession of his masterpiece and returned to Poland. "The Crucifixion," painted too large for the world to see, was rolled up and put in storage.

As the years passed, "The Crucifixion" was almost forgotten. Almost, but not quite. Its story, retold many times in artistic circles, finally reached the ears of the third man who was to decide the destiny of Styka's masterpiece. That man was Dr. Hubert Eaton, "The Builder" of Forest Lawn. It was in 1944 that Dr. Eaton, together with the Council of Regents, obtained the painting for Forest Lawn. Then followed the building of The Hall of The Crucifixion.

At last, on March 23—Good Friday—in 1951, The Hall of The Crucifixion was dedicated and "The Crucifixion" was unveiled to the world. Today it is shown to all who come seeking the true meaning of Christianity.

Those who visit The Hall of The Crucifixion will walk in renewed faith in Christ with these words ringing in their hearts:

> "For God so loved the world
> that He gave His only begotten Son,
> that whosoever believeth in Him
> should not perish, but have everlasting Life."

At Forest Lawn the last chapter of this magnificent, this awe-inspiring masterpiece has been written.

Martha (19), the sister of Lazarus. On her knees just in front, is Mary Magdalene (20), a woman abandoned to despair. Her long red hair unbound, she prays for a miracle to avert the ruthless sentence of His death.

The center of these conflicting emotions, Jesus stands alone. At His feet lie the scarlet robe, the crown of thorns, and the reed with which His persecutors mocked Him. His eyes, expressing faith, not fear, He stands looking to His Father in Heaven for strength to endure the ordeal of the Cross. Now—at this moment—civilization stands still. The world is at a crossroads. Revenge and hatred seem to have conquered the forgiveness and infinite love that Christ was born on earth to reveal. Yet from the lowering clouds of this appalling day will rise triumphant the Sun of Resurrection, bringing with it a message of salvation for all men who believe in Christ's promise of Eternal Life.

stand the two thieves, Gesmas (8) and Dismas (9), who will be crucified with Christ.

Between the crosses in the foreground crouch three of the executioners (10). The fourth (14), at the extreme right, has just unearthed a bone fulfilling an ancient prophecy that the Saviour would be crucified on the spot where Adam was buried.

Kneeling in the center background close to the Master is the burly farmer, Simon of Cyrene (12), who was forced to carry the cross of Jesus to the hill of Calvary.

Most pitiful of all who have climbed the hill today is the little family group which includes Mary (16), the mother of Jesus. She has suppressed her own anguish to lend what comfort she can to her Son in this dreadful hour. Next to her, comforting her, is the beloved disciple, John (15). To her left stand the wife of Cleophas (17), Lazarus (18) and

So skillfully did Jan Styka compose his gigantic painting that, despite the multitude of figures and vast area, all eyes focus immediately upon the central character, Jesus. A detail of the painting shows the Saviour at that

moment of suspense just before the crucifixion when He has met and overcome the excruciating mental agony that exceeds all physical suffering. The death that awaits Him loses its terror in a supreme triumph of faith.

From the Gospel According to St. Luke

And Pilate, when he had called together the chief priests and the rulers and the people,

Said unto them, Ye have brought this man unto me, as one that perverteth the people: and, behold, I, having examined *him* before you, have found no fault in this man touching those things whereof ye accuse him . . .

Pilate therefore, willing to release Jesus, spake again to them.

But they cried, saying, Crucify *him*, crucify him . . . And the voices of them and the chief priests prevailed.

And Pilate gave sentence that it should be as they required . . . he delivered Jesus to their will.

And as they led him away, they laid hold upon one Simon, a Cyrenian, coming out of the country, and on him they laid the cross, that he might bear it after Jesus . . .

And there were also two other, malefactors, led with him to be put to death.

And when they were come to the place, which is called Calvary, there they crucified him, and the malefactors, one on the right hand, and the other on the left.

Details of "The Crucifixion": Top, left background, Simon of Cyrene kneels by Stephanus the Warrant Officer; center foreground, Fourth Executioner; right of the cross, the Lictor bearing on his shoulder the fasces, symbol of authority; the Praetor, Roman administrator of justice. Below, left, Annas the high priest in red robe; foreground, Caiaphus in brown robe, Malchus in blue robe and three of the Executioners; right background, the two thieves, Gesmas and Dismas.

The Crucifixion

Then said Jesus. Father, forgive them; for they know not what they do.

And they parted his raiment, and cast lots.

And the people stood beholding . . . and the soldiers also mocked him, coming to him and offering him vinegar . . .

And one of the malefactors which were hanged railed on him, saying, If thou be Christ, save thyself and us.

But the other answering rebuked him, saying, Dost not thou fear God, seeing thou art in the same condemnation?

And we indeed justly; for we receive the due reward of our deeds: but this man hath done nothing amiss.

And he said unto Jesus, Lord, remember me when thou comest into thy kingdom.

And Jesus said unto him, Verily I say unto thee, Today shalt thou be with me in paradise.

And it was about the sixth hour, and there was a darkness over all the earth until the ninth hour.

And the sun was darkened, and the veil of the temple was rent in the midst.

And when Jesus had cried with a loud voice, he said, Father, into thy hands I commend my spirit.

Details of "The Crucifixion": Top, left to right, the Virgin Mary, John, the wife of Cleophas, Lazarus, Martha the sister of Lazarus, and Mary Magdalene. Center, extreme left background, Joseph of Arimathea and Nicodemus with retinue of servants; center foreground, Saul of Tarsus and Gameliel. Below, left background, Longinus the Centurion mounted on his white stallion; right foreground, directly behind donkey, Peter staring at the cock fluttering at his feet.

DR. HUBERT EATON
"THE BUILDER" AND FOUNDER OF
FOREST LAWN MEMORIAL-PARK

Biographical Sketch from "Who's Who in America"

EATON, Hubert, bus. exec., met. engr., art patron; b. Liberty, Mo., June 3, 1881; s. Prof. James Rodolphus and Martha (Lewright) E.; m. Anna Munger-Henderson, Dec. 10, 1918; 1 son, Roy. A.B. William Jewell Coll. Research and asst. chief chemist Boston & Mont. Consol. Copper Co. (now Anaconda Copper Co.), Great Falls, Mont.; chief chemist, Teziutlan Copper Co., Mexico; gen. mgr. Adaven Mining & Smelting Co., Nev.; chmn. advisory bd. Bank of America, Glendale, Calif.; founder & bd. chmn. Am. Sec. & Fidelity Corp., Forest Lawn Co., Forest Lawn Life Insur. Co., Council of Regents. Mem. Ct. of Honor. Originated (1916) the "Memorial-Park Plan" which has revolutionized cemeteries throughout U.S., and in exemplification thereof founded and built Forest Lawn Memorial-Park noted for its first substitution of tombstones with bronze tablets set level with the lawn; great collections of large-sized works of famous European and American sculptors, and stained glass; Moretti recreation in stained glass of Leonardo da Vinci's "Last Supper," Jan Styka's immense painting "The Crucifixion," and three famous old-world churches, etc. Author of pamphlets on cemetery development. Knighted Order Crown of Italy (1932) by King Victor Emanuel III, Star of Solidarity (1951) by Pres. of Italian Republic. Trustee William Jewell Coll. and Redlands University. Associate of Caltech, Occ. Coll., Pomona Coll. LL.D., L.H.D., A.F.A.C. (Italy), F.R.S.A. (Great Britain). Vice-pres. Boy Scouts of America, Los Angeles area. Memb. Soc. S.R., Colonial Wars, Sigma Nu, Alpha Phi Gamma. Baptist, Mason (K.T. Shriner). Clubs: California, Jonathan, Los Angeles Country, Beverly, Aliso Gun, La Grulla Gun. Home: 837 Greenway Drive, Beverly Hills, Calif. Summer: 2000 East Bay Front, Balboa, Calif.

The Council of Regents

of

Memorial Court of Honor of Forest Lawn Memorial-Park

May 1, 1955

Composed of outstanding business and professional men, Forest Lawn's Council of Regents advises on all matters concerning the growth of the Memorial-Park as a cultural center of religion and fine arts.

Bottom Row	*Middle Row*	*Top Row*
Frederick Llewellyn, *Secretary*	M. M. Kauffman	Herman Psenner
John F. Huber	C. L. Peck	John Randle Moore
Dr. Rufus B. von KleinSmid, *V. Chairman*	Daniel P. Bryant	LeRoy M. Edwards
Dr. Hubert Eaton, *Chairman*	Harold Morrison	Dr. Willard W. Keith
Bishop Gerald H. Kennedy, *Chaplain*	Jean Hersholt	Justice W. Turney Fox
Dr. Edgar J. Goodspeed	Walter Braunschweiger	Dr. Arthur G. Coons
Fred H. Jones	Dr. Orris E. Jackson	H. M. Burgwald
	Paul R. Watkins	

FOREST LAWN-HOLLYWOOD HILLS is the extended fulfillment of Dr. Hubert Eaton's "Memorial-Park Plan." Standing in warm invitation at the entrance to its 450 acres of gently rolling vistas and green lawns is the combined Mortuary and Administration Building—a stately structure of the gracious Colonial-American period. This is the promise that whatever place bears the honored name of Forest Lawn shall grow in beauty through "The Builder's" concept; the concept that inspiration, peace, solace, and the witness to Eternal Life may be found in enduring beauty and Service to the Living.

AN ATMOSPHERE of hope and confidence pervades the Hollywood Hills Mortuary. Its pleasant slumber rooms are unlike any ever provided for those who seek communion with their loved ones. Like any comfortable home, where colors accent and brighten familiar surroundings, these rooms are tastefully decorated in cheerful, heartwarming colors. Easy chairs, covered with warm chintzes—lounges, upholstered in rich fabrics—walls, hued in pastel loveliness—even the rare prints . . . all help to ease the burden of heavy hearts. A few steps away down a pleasant corridor is the lovely Chapel serving all creeds. Decorated in luxurious simplicity, it offers comforting solace through its intimate tranquility.

A SHRINE of memory where beauty lifts the heart, Forest Lawn-Hollywood Hills adjoins Griffith Park in San Fernando Valley. Standing on three sides in protective might are the high rugged hills for which it is named. Their quiet slopes, heavily wooded with venerable Live Oaks and other beautiful native trees, meet verdant lawns bright with sunlight. This is the incomparable natural setting for the memorial art treasures, lovely churches and quiet gardens which are to give Forest Lawn-Hollywood Hills the distinctive beauty and meaning which have placed Forest Lawn in Glendale above any cemetery the world has ever known.

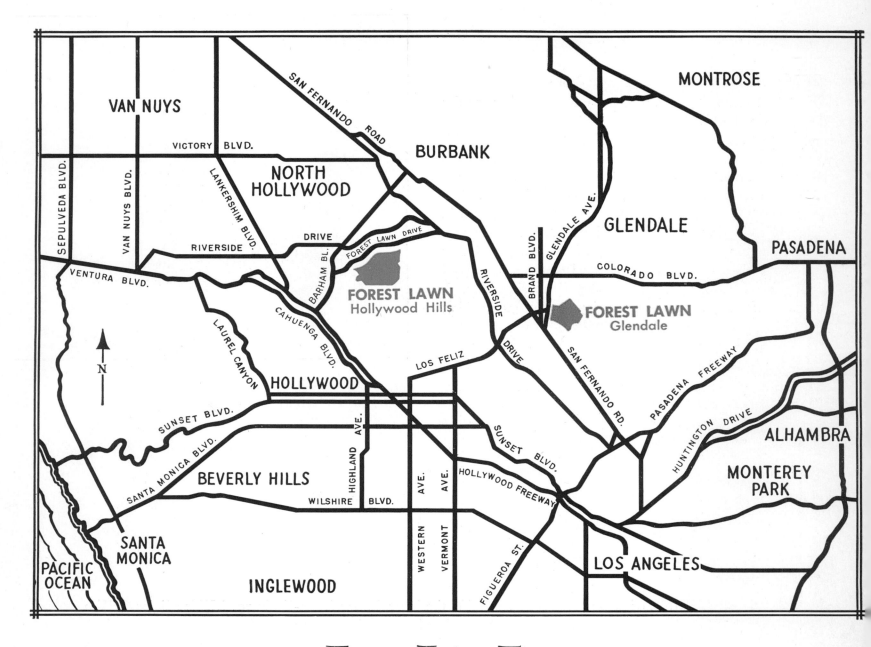

Forest Lawn Facts

Forest Lawn Memorial-Park

FOREST LAWN, the world's first and only true Memorial-Park, is internationally famous as an art center and as America's outstanding cemetery property. The revolutionary Memorial-Park Plan of cemetery development, conceived and realized by Dr. Hubert Eaton, the Founder of Forest Lawn Memorial-Park, has won acclaim throughout the world for its philosophy of hope and its witness to Eternal Life.

Forest Lawn Hollywood Hills

And while the original Memorial-Park in Glendale grows ever more inspiringly lovely in landscape, architecture and art, a new area of remarkable natural beauty has been added, the gates of which are less than 15 minutes' drive. This is Forest Lawn-Hollywood Hills at the edge of the San Fernando Valley, adjacent to Los Angeles' Griffith Park. The first structure here is the stately Mortuary-Administration Building of Georgian Colonial American architecture. At Hollywood Hills, mortuary and cemetery combine to provide everything in one place at time of sorrow, in the same high traditions of Forest Lawn Memorial-Park.

Art Treasures

Forest Lawn contains hundreds of art treasures and architectural masterpieces, including:
The majestic Memorial Court of Honor;
The renowned Moretti re-creation in stained glass of Leonardo da Vinci's painting, "The Last Supper," truly the outstanding art contribution of the present generation to posterity;

America's finest collection of stained glass;
The only place in the world where replicas of Michelangelo's greatest works are assembled;
The noted "Mystery of Life" statuary group and the Mystery of Life Garden; many other inspiring features, details of which will be found in the Forest Lawn Art Guide.

Famous Churc

The Little Church of the Flowers, the Wee Kirk o' the Heather, and the Church of the Recessional reproduce three famous old-world churches, while the Church of the Hills at Hollywood Hills was designed from the 18th century First Parish Church of Portland, Maine. More than 42,000 persons have been married in Forest Lawn churches.

The Hall of T Crucifixion

Thousands of visitors pilgrimage to The Hall of The Crucifixion, a massive building atop Mount Forest Lawn. Within is enshrined Jan Styka's "The Crucifixion," America's largest religious painting.

Visitors

Reverent visitors come from all over the world to view the famous works of art and to enjoy the comforting atmosphere of peace and beauty at Forest Lawn.

Educational

Schools send their classes to Forest Lawn to study the things of which they read in textbooks concerning literature, history, art, architecture, engineering and construction. Women's clubs and men's organizations come for group study and inspiration. This great art center enriches the cultural life of the entire community.

Civic Asset Forest Lawn is widely recognized as a civic asset, a world-famous shrine of beauty, culture and spiritual value.

Park Idea Forest Lawn originated and developed the Memorial-Park Plan for cemeteries. Instead of grotesque tombstones, it provides memorials in the form of inspiring marble statuary and distinctive memorial tablets set level with the lawn.

Protection Protecting ranges of hills set both Forest Lawn locations apart from the world about them. Forest Lawn-Glendale also is surrounded by an eight-foot wall, with the largest set of wrought-iron gates in the world. Both the undertaking establishments and the mausoleum are Class-I steel and concrete buildings, resistant to fire and earthquake.

Permanent Improvements All improvements are of the most permanent character. As an example of the way Forest Lawn builds, the Great Mausoleum contains thousands of tons of steel and concrete and its foundations go as deep as 33 feet into solid rock.

Assurance of Future The Endowment Care Fund amounts to more than three million dollars and increases steadily each year. It is estimated that the Fund will eventually exceed twenty million dollars. Only the interest can be used for general care and maintenance; the principal can never be expended.

Size Forest Lawn-Glendale comprises more than three hundred acres and has 8 miles of paved roads with curbs; 80 miles of underground water systems and drains; 28 buildings, 10,000 trees and over 100,000 shrubs. At Hollywood Hills, the area initially developed with lawns, trees, roads, water pipes, storm drains, and protective fencing consists of about sixty acres.

Interments There are now more than 155,000 interments in these two locations, increasing at the rate of approximately 6,500 per year.

Employees Forest Lawn employs from 700 to 800 people.

Low Prices Combining undertaking with all forms of interment in one place and under one management reduces overhead and makes low prices possible.

Complete Service Forest Lawn offers complete undertaking service and all forms of interment (cemetery, mausoleum, cremation and inurnment) in one sacred place, under one management, with one convenient credit arrangement for everything.

Pictorial Map OF **FOREST LAWN** GLENDALE